Y0-BGE-459

Earth, Stars, and Writers

Philip Levine,
Orlando Patterson,
and
Norman Rush

Library of Congress
Washington
1992

The publication of this book was made possible through private contributions to the Center for the Book and the National Book Foundation.

Library of Congress Cataloging-in-Publication Data

Levine, Philip, 1928–
    Earth, stars, and writers / Philip Levine, Orlando Patterson, and Norman Rush.
        p.   cm. — (The National Book Week lectures)
    "Presented during National Book Week 1992 by the winners of the 1991 National Book Awards"—P. v.
    Includes bibliographical references.
    Contents: Entering poetry / Philip Levine — About freedom / Orlando Patterson — The writing life / Norman Rush.
    ISBN 0-8444-0771-2 (alk. paper)
—— —— Copy 3 Z663.118 .E2 1992
    1. Authors, American—20th century—Biography. 2. Authors and readers—United States. 3. Books and reading—United States. 4. Authorship. I. Patterson, Orlando, 1940– . II. Rush, Norman. III. Title. IV. Series.
PS129.L48 1992
810.9'0054—dc20
                                      92-36089
                                        CIP

CONTENTS

Preface

John Y. Cole

Center for the Book

v

Introduction

Neil Baldwin

National Book Foundation

vii

Entering Poetry

Philip Levine

1

About Freedom

Orlando Patterson

13

The Writing Life

Norman Rush

25

PREFACE

These three talks, presented during National Book Week 1992 by the winners of the 1991 National Book Awards, Philip Levine, Orlando Patterson, and Norman Rush, continue a partnership and a published lecture series that has reached its third volume. The partners are the Center for the Book in the Library of Congress and the National Book Foundation, which sponsors the National Book Awards. This joint enterprise stems from a common goal: to stimulate public awareness and appreciation of books, writers, and the values of a literate and creative society. National Book Week, celebrated the third week of January each year, is a weeklong celebration of American books and writers which features writers talking about their writing. The Center for the Book and the National Book Foundation invite libraries, schools, universities, and other groups to mark National Book Week each January by inviting a local writer to discuss the "writing life."

Philip Levine, who began publishing poetry in 1955, won the 1991 National Book Award for poetry for his book *What Work Is*. His talk was presented on January 23, 1992, at the California State Library in Sacramento under the auspices of the California Center for the Book, one of the many affiliates of the Center for the Book in the Library of Congress. Mr. Levine's contribution is especially welcome since it is the first National Book Award presented for poetry since 1983. Sociologist

Orlando Patterson, whose book *Freedom* won the award for nonfiction, spoke at the Library of Congress—also on January 23, 1992. On May 15, he spoke in Lansing, Michigan, at a program sponsored by the Michigan Center for the Book. Norman Rush won the 1991 National Book Award for his novel *Mating*. His talk was presented on March 4, 1992, at a program sponsored in Philadelphia by the Pennsylvania Center for the Book.

The Center for the Book and the National Book Foundation wish to express their appreciation to the Lila Wallace–Reader's Digest Fund for its support of National Book Week and the "Writing Life" program, which brought National Book Award winners and finalists to communities throughout America in 1992. In addition to Philip Levine, Orlando Patterson, and Norman Rush, the speakers were John Casey, Ron Chernow, Muriel Feelings, Paula Fox, Ellen Gilchrist, Gail Godwin, Madeleine L'Engle, Howard Norman, Richard Rhodes, and Sandra Scofield. Ten state centers for the book hosted writers. In addition to California, Michigan, and Pennsylvania, they were the state centers of Florida, Illinois, Iowa, Kansas, Minnesota, Nebraska, and Oklahoma.

The Center for the Book in the Library of Congress was established in 1977 to stimulate public interest in books, reading, and libraries and to encourage the study of the role of print culture in shaping our society. The projects of the Center for the Book, its state affiliates, and its organizational partners are funded by tax-deductible contributions from individuals, corporations, and foundations.

John Y. Cole
Director
The Center for the Book

INTRODUCTION

Gertrude Stein wrote about "how writing is written," but her rhetoric was too complex to demystify the process. Then again, elucidation was not her purpose. In the form itself she set forth intentionally to demonstrate and confirm just how hard it was to compose language. Intrepid and dogmatic, Stein preached to the converted; her audience was small, intellectually attuned, but not always sympathetic.

Many decades later, the National Book Foundation has likewise set itself the mission to explain "how writing is written," but in an utterly different cultural setting, to widely varying audiences all across America, in settlement houses, schools, libraries, art museums, bookstores, and community centers. National Book Award winners and finalists representing a distinguished literary tradition that began when the award was established in 1950 are speaking about their work—not merely giving readings—and revealing their writing lives in all their mystery, grace, and labor.

In the past three years since this ambitious and necessary outreach program was launched, more than seventy-five noted authors have visited twenty states and Washington, D.C., under the auspices of the Foundation. The three 1991 National Book Award winners represented here joined the Foundation's public literacy crusade with enthusiasm, and we are pleased to publish their remarks delivered during National

Book Week in January 1992 as part of our annual partnership monograph series with the Center for the Book in the Library for Congress.

Poet—and, one must add, philosopher—Philip Levine tells us how he "entered poetry," presenting vignettes as metaphors culled from a lifetime of inspired observation. Levine's sensual engagement with the phenomenal world around him began in childhood, before he was even fully aware of the implications of his blessing (or curse). Every thing matters to him; every person he encounters along the way brings baggage of significance; every dream is taken seriously. And beneath the panoply of situations enveloping the poet resides the acknowledgment and acceptance of mystery.

Orlando Patterson moves eloquently outward from the informing concept of his work-in-progress, tracing back to the roots of the idea for *Freedom*—a revelation that the very notion of being free began in the mind of the enslaved. By turns intellectually graceful and personally evocative, Patterson opens many doors: to his profession of sociology; to his Caribbean landscape; to the feeling of being black. Patterson is fearless in revealing that his thesis took shape in a Jamaican dialectic, a struggle embedded in his culture, which then had to be forcefully wrestled with for many, many years.

The crucial motif of self-awareness recurs in Norman Rush's ruminative essay. Here is a sensibility in which sophisticated, ever-so-slightly ironic insight is exploited, the result of the author's ability to step back from himself before fashioning sentences. Norman Rush tells us that he was in effect a *writer* long before he became an *author*. It was not a case of always wanting to be a writer, but, rather, of simply existing as one. Growing up in a household surrounded by books and with a father who was an incipient writer left its indelible and inescapable mark on Rush's psyche.

We suspect common denominators, and with good reason, when we write of writers, because we respect singular voices. Good style preserves its uniqueness by avoiding definition, but we feel it keenly and it brings us pleasure. Suffice it to say that here are three (thankfully) very different writers who found words early, trusted language as the best path, and discovered ways to integrate surrender with mastery.

Neil Baldwin
Executive Director
The National Book Foundation

ENTERING POETRY

During and after dinner there were always arguments at my house: my older brother Eli and my mother against my twin brother Eddie and me. Eli was sixteen and wore a clean starched shirt and tie to the table; he frequently complained about our manners, our language, and our filthy fingernails. He ate methodically and used his napkin often, making little pats at his lips. He also ate a great deal, so the meals seemed to go on forever. It was no good racing through dinner because we were required to remain until the meal was completed. It was also useless to go to my room after dinner because Eddie's single preoccupation was with getting revenge. His favorite phrase was, "I'll give no quarter and take no quarter." (He'd already discovered Sir Walter Scott.) I'd seen him fight often and knew he was serious. When he got another boy down he would kick him with all his considerable might. Only the tallest and toughest of the Episcopal boys at our new school still called him a dirty Jew.

The year was 1940. My mother had just purchased a house near the outskirts of Detroit located on an almost empty block. There was a similar square two-storied house on each side of ours and two houses directly across from ours and from the house of Steve Psaris, our neighbor to the north. There was also one house directly behind ours. To the east were two blocks of fields and then Livernois Avenue, famous for its profusion of used-car lots. To the west were two totally

1

undeveloped blocks, still deeply wooded with maple, elm, and beech and thick underbrush. In my imagination this settlement of six families was a tiny America, an outpost of civilization between a vast open prairie and the mysterious darkness of a wilderness.

When I sneaked out of the house after dinner each night I headed directly for the security of the dense thickets and trees. Once into the woods I would make my way to one of my favorite trees, most often a large copper beech whose low branches spread out almost horizontally, and lean back and survey the night sky. There was no industry in this part of the city, and so the stars were visible and on some nights spectacular. One night I began to speak both to and of them. Immediately I felt something enormously satisfying about this speaking, perhaps because nothing came back in the form of an argument. It was utterly unlike any speaking I'd either heard or made before. I liked the way my voice, which was just changing—for I was twelve—would gather itself around or within certain sounds, the *r* of "rains," the long open *o* sound of "moon." I would say "rain" and "moon" in the same sentence, hear them echo each other, and a shiver of delight would pass through me. On cloudy, starless nights when the air seemed dense and close, I'd hurl my new voice out at the sky by saying, "The clouds obscure the stars," one tiny delicious sentence, but for the most part I was not brief. Best were those nights after a hard rain. In the darkness the smell of the wet earth would fill my head almost to the bursting point. "The damp earth is giving birth," I would say, and then in sentence after sentence I'd go on to list all that was being born within and outside me, though in the dense night I could hardly discern where I ended and the rest of the world began.

I was no longer addressing the stars, for often they had deserted me. Was I addressing God? I'm sure I was not, for I had no belief in a God who could hear me even though I was learning Hebrew and reading the Bible and discussing its deeper meanings each week with my instructor, a chubby-handed little man who was preparing himself for the rabbinate. Quite simply, Eddie and I had worked it out together and come to a complete accord: there was no God or any chosen people. "What the fuck were we chosen for?" Eddie would shout out after one of our frequent losing battles with the taller Episcopalians, most of whom were driven to school in long Lincolns or Packards, while we made the mile-and-a-half trek on foot even in the worst weather. No, I believe I was already a blooming Platonist addressing the complement, all that I was not and yearned to become. When I was in the crow's nest of my copper beech the wet earth smells rose around me and the wind quivered the hard leaves and carried my voice out to the edges of the night; I could almost believe someone was listening and that each of my words freighted with feeling truly mattered. I was certain I was becoming a man.

One spring day, returning from school through the great prairie east of our house, I came across a wild iris, a tiny purple thing growing on its own, just a single bloom with no sign of a neighbor, doing its solitary best to enlighten the afternoon. I ran home and returned with a bucket and shovel from the garage. I dug up the iris, making sure to take plenty of dirt and being careful not to sever the roots. In our backyard I dug up a few square feet of sod near the back fence and planted the wildflower. I watered it carefully, but even by dinnertime it looked as though it had had it, so pitifully did it sag. By morning it was a goner. On Saturday I combed the open fields and found two more wild irises. I dug a second hole and planted the two side by side, this time preparing the ground with a dark, evil-smelling fertilizer I'd bought at Cunningham's Drug Store. I watered one flower hardly at all for fear I might have drowned the first iris. By later afternoon it was clear they'd both died. I asked the advice of Sophie Psaris, Steve's wife, who seemed able to make anything grow. She assured me that not even she could transplant a wildflower and make it grow. As a girl in Salonika,

3

she'd fallen in love with the blood red poppies that stained the meadows each April, but through she'd tried to get them to take hold in her mother's garden, she'd always failed. "Try rosebushes," she said. "The flowers are beautiful and they grow easily." I decided there was something proper about the irises' stubborn refusal to grow inside our fenced yard, something dignified in their preferring death to captivity. Never again would I interfere.

A week later with money earned from washing windows, I bought my first rosebush, a little thorny stick of a thing with its dirt-encrusted roots wrapped in burlap. "You want something that will grow like mad?" said Bert, the little wizened Englishman who worked in the garden section of Cunningham's. For sixty-nine cents he let me have a mock orange. In no time at all, he assured me, it would be taller than I, but then I was still less than five feet tall. "Why do you call it a mock orange?" I asked. "Because that's its name. You see it doesn't give any oranges; you can't grow oranges this far north. It's not even a tree; it's a shrub, but the blossoms look and smell like real orange blossoms."

The instructions for planting the rose spoke of "sandy loam" and the need to place the roots six to nine inches deep into this "sandy loam." After my disasters with the irises, I was hesitant and so took a handful of our backyard dirt to show Sophie. "Is this sandy loam?" I asked. She took a pinch from my open palm between her thumb and forefinger and smelled it and then put a few grains on her tongue and spit them out. "Pheelip," she said in her heavily accented English, "this is just dirt, you know, dirt that comes from the ground." This didn't really answer my question, so with no little trepidation I took a second handful to Cunningham's to show Bert. Was this in fact sandy loam? He stared at me in silence for half a minute and then cocked his head to one side. Why was I asking? I explained how the instructions had spoken of a six- to nine-inch hole in "sandy loam." "Where'd you get this?" he said. I told him I'd dug it out of a hole in my back yard. "Yes, of course you did," he said, "it's dirt, it'll do just fine. Call it 'sandy loam' if you'd like." He assured me that if I just planted the thing in a hole and gave it some water it would grow. "It's a lot less fussy than we are," he added.

Somewhat heartened, I returned home and planted the mock orange in the already fertilized hole that had failed the iris and planted the rose beside the fence separating our lot from Steve Psaris's driveway. I liked the way my hands smelled afterward. I washed away the grosser signs of their filthiness, but I was cautious to leave just enough dirt under my fingernails so that whenever I wanted to I could catch a whiff of the earth's curious pungency that suggested both tobacco and rust. Though the soil of our backyard was a dull gray brown, the perfume was a foxy red. For once, I looked forward to Eli's complaints.

The rose especially was such a sad little thing that in spite of Bert's encouragement I was certain it would not survive, but within a week tiny reddish twigs began to jut out from the woody gray stick. I would press my thumb against the new thorns just to feel their sharpness against my skin. Eddie liked to speak of something he called a "blood oath," a vow taken by two strong men and sealed by the mixing of their blood. At the time he was reading Dumas and Sabatini and often spoke also of taking fencing lessons, though we knew no one in Detroit who gave them. One day I considered puncturing my skin against the largest of the thorns, but I stopped short of this gesture. Sophie had assured me the buds would come as they had on their bushes. I knew from watching them they would transform themselves from hard green almond-shaped stones to the swelling red-tipped about-to-be-flowers.

One late May morning, I glanced out of the back window of the breakfast nook to discover the mock orange in bloom. Caught up in the excitement of the beginning of the baseball season, I'd not been paying attention and was taken by surprise. There were suddenly more than a dozen tiny blossoms and a rich, deep perfume that reminded me of the perfume of my Aunt Belle, my mother's younger sister. After school I cut a small branch of three blossoms and placed it in a glass of water and set it in the middle of the dining room table. To my surprise, that evening no one noticed it, and dinner passed with Eli discussing his plans for a camping trip in northern Canada. I listened in silence, and when the others had left the table I dropped the little branch down the front of my shirt.

The days were lengthening, and it was still light out when I sneaked out of the house after helping with the dishes. I made my way to the deepest center of the woods and climbed a young maple tree and gazed up into the deepening sky above. I must have dozed off for a few minutes because quite suddenly the stars emerged in a blacker sky. Although I did not know their names—in fact, I did not even know they had names—I began to address them quietly, for I never spoke with "full-throated ease" until hidden by the cover of total darkness. A soft wind shook the leaves around me. From my own hands I caught the smell of earth and iron, which now I carried with me at all times. I reached down my shirt and extracted the mock orange branch and breathed in the deep feminine odors while between thumb and forefinger I fretted the blossoms until they fell apart. I began then to address my own hands, which seemed somehow to have been magically transformed into earth. For the first time a part of me became my night words, for now the darkness was complete. "These hands have entered the ground from which they sprang," I said, and tasting the words I immediately liked them and repeated them, and then more words came that also seemed familiar and right. Then I looked on the work my hands had wrought, then I said in my heart, as it happened to the gardener, so it happened to me, for we all go into one place; we are all earth and return to earth. The dark was everywhere, and as my voice went out I was sure it reached the edges of creation. I was sure too my words must have smelled of sandy loam and orange blossoms. That was the first night of my life I entered poetry.

★　　★　　★

In the spring of 1952 in Detroit, I was working at Chevy Gear and Axle, the "abandoned factory" of a poem in my first book, *On the Edge,* and I hated the job more than any I'd had before or have had since, not only because it was so hard, the work so heavy and monotonous that after an hour or two I was sure each night that I would never last the shift, but also because it was dangerous. There in the forge room, where I worked until I was somehow promoted to a less demanding, equally boring job, the stock we handled so gingerly with tongs was still red-hot as we pulled it from the gigantic presses and hung it above us on conveyors that carried our handiwork out of sight. Others had mastered the art of handling the tongs loosely, the way a good tennis player handles his racquet as he approaches the net for a drop volley, applying just enough pressure not to let go and not enough to choke it. Out of fear I squeezed for all I was worth, and all the good advice, the coaching I received from my fellow workers, was of no use.

One night just after we'd returned to our machines after the twenty-minute break, the guy I was working with—a squat, broad-shouldered young black man whose energy and good spirits I'd admired for weeks—tapped me on the shoulder and indicated with a gesture that I should step aside. Together we'd been manning a small punch press; he handed me the stock that came along a conveyor, I inserted it in the machine, had it punched, and then hung it on another conveyor. On this occasion he said nothing, though even if he had I wouldn't have heard him over "the oceanic roar of work." He withdrew a short-handled sledgehammer from inside his shirt, and gripping it with both hands hammered furiously at the press's die. He then inserted a piece of stock in the machine, tripped the button that brought the press down, and leaped aside before the press could whip the metal out of his hands. The press froze. I went to summon the foreman, Lonnie, while my partner

7

disposed of the hammer. Lonnie took one look at the machine and summoned two men senior to him, or so I assumed since they arrived dressed in business suits. For twenty minutes they searched the area. I finally figured out that they were looking for the instrument with which the press had been sabotaged. Then they separated us and grilled me. There was no question, they assured me, that the press bore the marks of violence. What had "the nigger" done? I answered that I'd seen nothing out of the ordinary, the machine just broke down, almost tore my hands apart. Oh, they looked at each other, I wanted it that way. Well, they could certainly accommodate me. Before the night was over, I was back on the "Big Press," handling those red-hot sections of steel, my hands stiffening and kinking inside the huge gauntlets. Within a few days I was once again dreaming of fire as my hands gnarled even in sleep. I lasted a few more weeks and when it became obvious that the "Big Press" was mine forever, I quit.

Five years later, while living in Palo Alto, California, on a writing grant from Stanford University, I received an article clipped from a Detroit newspaper and mailed to me. It told of the closing of Chevy Gear and Axle; its functions had been moved to a new, highly automated plant near Pontiac. I had already tried at least a dozen times to capture the insane, nightmarish quality of my life at Chevy: that epic clanging of steel on steel, the smell of the dead rats we poisoned who crawled off into their secret places and gained a measure of revenge, the freezing winds at our backs as winter moved through the broken windows, the awesome heat in our faces, those dreamlike moments when the lights failed and we stood in darkness and the momentary silence of the stilled machines. In the springlike winter of 1957, sitting in the little poetry room of the Stanford library, which was mine alone each morning, half a country and a universe away from Chevy, I could recall almost without hatred that old sense of utter weariness that descended each night from my neck to my shoulders, and then down my arms to my wrists and hands, and how as the weeks had passed my body had changed, thickening as though the muscles and tendons had permanently swelled, so that I carried what I did with me at all times, even when I lifted a pencil to write my poems. It was not the thickening heaviness of myself I tried to capture in my abandoned factory poem—I only managed a glimmer of that—for I was determined to say something about the importance of the awfulness I had shared in and observed around me, a worthy aim, certainly, but one that stopped me from writing the poetry of what I had most deeply and personally experienced.

Seven years later in the spring of 1964, I was living in a large airy house in Fresno, California, a house of beautiful slow dawns. Each morning I would waken early, before six, and watch the light—yellow and pale green as it filtered through the leaves of the sycamore outside my bedroom—transform the darkness into fact, clear and precise, from the tiled floor to the high, sloping, unfinished wooden ceiling. It was a real California house. I would rise, toss on a bathrobe, and work at my poems for hours seated at the kitchen table, work until the kids rising for school broke my concentration. To be accurate, I would work unless the morning were spoiled by some uncontrollable event, like a squadron of jet fighters slamming suddenly over the low roofs of the neighborhood, for we lived less than a quarter mile from a National Guard airfield.

One morning in April of that year I awakened distressed by a dream, one that I cannot call a nightmare, for nothing violent or terribly unpleasant had occurred in it. I dreamed that I'd received a phone call from a man I'd known in Detroit, Eugene Watkins, a black man with whom I'd worked for some years in a grease shop there. Eugene was a tall, slender man, ten years older than I, and although he had his difficulties at home he rarely spoke of them. In fact he rarely spoke. What I remember most clearly about working beside him was that I never liked schlepping or loading or unloading in tandem with him because he had a finger missing on his left hand, and I had some deep-seated fear that whatever

9

had caused that loss could easily recur, and I didn't want the recurrence to take some treasured part of myself. The dream was largely a phone conversation, one in which I could see Eugene calling from a phone booth beside U.S. 99 in Bakersfield, 120 miles south of where I lived. He'd called to tell me he was in California with his wife and daughter. They'd driven all the way from Detroit and had just arrived. They wanted to know what they should do and see while they were in the West. As I babbled on about the charms of Santa Monica, L.A.'s Miracle Mile, the fashionable restaurants neither they nor I could afford, the scenic drive up U.S. 1 to Big Sur, I knew that what Eugene was actually seeking was an invitation to visit me. I even mentioned the glories of Yosemite and King's Canyon National Park—neither more than an hour from where I lived—and yet I never invited him. Finally he thanked me for all the information I'd given him, said goodbye, and quietly hung up. In the dream I saw him leave the phone booth and shamble, head down, back to the car, exactly as I would have in his place. I awakened furious with myself for my coldness, my lack of generosity, my snobbery. Why, I asked myself, had I behaved this way? Was it because Eugene was black? Several black friends had visited my house. Because he was working class? I was living in a largely working-class neighborhood. (Who else has an airfield at the end of the block?) Did I think I was so hot with my assistant professorship at a second-rate California college, with my terrific salary that was probably no more than Eugene earned? Was I trying to jettison my past and join the rising tide of intellectuals, car salesmen, TV repairmen, and bank managers who would make it to the top? What the hell was I becoming?

It finally occurred to me that I had not rejected Eugene, my past, the city of my birth, or anything. I had had a dream, and that dream was a warning of what might happen to me if I rejected what I'd been and who I was. The kids were up and preparing for school, so I climbed back in bed with my yellow legal pad and my pen. I was in that magical state in which nothing could hurt me or sidetrack me; I had achieved that extraordinary level of concentration we call inspiration. When I closed my eyes and looked back into the past, I did not see the blazing color of the forges of nightmare or the torn faces of the workers. I didn't hear the deafening ring of metal on metal, or catch under everything the sweet stink of decay. Not on that morning. Instead I was myself in the company of men and women of enormous sensitivity, delicacy, consideration. I saw us touching each other emotionally and physically, hands upon shoulders, across backs, faces pressed to faces. We spoke to each other out of the deepest centers of our need, and we listened. In those terrible places designed to rob us of our bodies and our spirits, we sustained each other.

The first lines I wrote were for Eugene Watkins. I imagined us together in the magical, rarified world of poetry, the world I knew we would never enter. Although it's snowing there, when we leave the car to enter the unearthly grove, no snow falls on our hair or on the tops of our shoes because "It's the life of poems; / the boughs expansive, our feet dry." But of course that was not the world I was returning to; I wanted to capture in my poetry the life Eugene and I had shared, so before the poem ("In a Grove Again") ends, the grove transforms itself into any roadside stop where two guys might pause to take a piss:

> Meanwhile back in the car there are talismen:
>
> A heater, the splashed entrails of newspapers,
> A speedometer that glows and always reads 0.
> We have not come here to die. We are workers
> And have stopped to relieve ourselves, so we sigh.

I remained in bed much of that week. The poems were coming, and for reasons I couldn't explain, I felt my inspiration had something to do with the particular feel and odor of the bed. While there I wrote most of the Detroit poems that appear in my second book, *Not This Pig*. I believe that they were the first truly good poems I'd written about the city. They are by no means all sweetness and light. There was and still is much that I hate about Detroit, much that deserves to be hated, but I had somehow found a "balanced" way of writing about what I'd experienced; I'd tempered the violence I felt toward those who'd maimed and cheated me with a tenderness toward those who had touched and blessed me.

Philip Levine

A B O U T   F R E E D O M

I like the idea of the Center for the Book, and the sound of its name. It's such a muscular title, so forceful and to the point. I am very happy to be involved with its badly needed effort to promote reading, especially in light of its association with the National Book Foundation, an organization to which, as you might well imagine, I am extremely partial.

I was asked to talk about my personal experience with the writing life and how I came to write *Freedom*. Why did I choose this subject, what motivated me to spend so many years on it, and what particular set of concerns and anxieties aided or impeded its execution?

Every writer is, I suppose, motivated by a combination of two kinds of forces in pursuing his goal. There is the consciously motivated set of reasons, the facts which he thinks explain his desire to write. These are the ones he offers himself and those who probe, and which he is inclined to emphasize on occasions such as National Book Week lectures. They are not to be despised, in spite of our inclination to prefer the deeper, hidden causes in what is still too Freudian an age. Our rationalizations both comfort and impel us; sometimes they are indeed the really important reasons why we do the things we do. We should certainly resist the temptation to consider them less authentic. I will return to these shortly.

The subconscious reasons we come to know only on reflection, after the fact, sometimes recollected in tranquility, more often, at least with me, in sudden flashes during the turmoil of everyday life. We must be wary of these reasons, for they are too often feathers in the wind of one's changing moods. So take what I have to say about them later with a pinch of salt. I do believe what I will say is true now; but I might not next Thursday morning.

In the simplest terms, *Freedom* grew, consciously and directly, out of my earlier work. Perhaps I should say, my earlier works, for in many ways this work is the culmination of nearly everything I've previously written, including my works of fiction. The basic argument of the work is clearly anticipated in the last pages of my previous book, *Slavery and Social Death,* published in 1982. I had intended to write a sequel to that work, on the subject of slavery, but was so intrigued by what emerged in my final reflections that I abandoned the idea of another work on slavery and wrote instead a book which was really a long elaboration of those concluding reflections.

You see, in the course of writing about slavery I increasingly became aware of the fact that I was really writing about something else; I was, as it were, haunted by what I have called a ghost concept, one I was able to keep under wraps until I came to write the concluding chapter. At that point I allowed it to reveal itself and discovered that behind my exploration of the problem of slavery was the idea of freedom. As I indicated in the preface to my book on freedom, I had gone in search of killing a wolf called slavery, only to find myself in the tracks of the lamb called freedom, innocent, lovable freedom. This was too intriguing a discovery to put aside. So I suspended any further search on the nature of slavery and concentrated my efforts on this new, puzzling quarry.

I suspect that this sort of thing happens to many writers. The dogged pursuit of one problem poses, at the end, one or more questions that are both more troublesome and more intriguing than the problem that led to it. It is certainly true that the most important part of any successful writing project is the nature of the question that inspired it. I was fortunate in having just such an interesting question emerging from the last pages of my previous work.

The basic question then was why was freedom so perversely associated with slavery, man's greatest inhumanity to man? The audacious answer that came, reluctantly, was that the association was not accidental but fundamental, indeed genetic. From this emerged the further realization that we have posed the problem of slavery and freedom the wrong way around; that is to say, we have tended to define slavery as the absence of freedom, assuming freedom to be the natural, universal condition. I came to realize that it was slavery which was the more natural institution, the one which was more universal. The problem to be explained was not slavery but what now seemed unusual: freedom.

This turning around of the way we normally see things is another important aspect of a successful writing project. The truth, at least in social life, is often hidden in the inverted causal sequence which history and ideology impose on our most cherished beliefs. Generations of historians, for example, were only too willing to be seduced by the Tocquevillian notion that it was America's commitment to equality that accounted for its great economic vitality and abundance. The truth, historians have only recently come to realize, was that Tocqueville was writing at a time when America was at its most inegalitarian. He had gotten it all wrong; and indeed the situation was to get worse as America grew richer. Only then did America start to become the egalitarian paradise he thought he saw. The truth was the reverse of what history and ideology had imposed on our way of thinking: America, like other industrial societies, became more equal only because of, and after, the brutal process of becoming prosperous.

And so it was with freedom. Man was not born free and then found himself everywhere in chains, as Rousseau so famously thought. Rather, men and women found themselves in chains, and, not everywhere, but in a certain part of the world, constructed the value and idea of freedom. What is more, the relationship was not a simple negation, but a generative contradiction. This is another important lesson about social life first discovered by Heraclitus in ancient Greece and reformulated in modern times by Hegel and Marx: that life does not emerge in simple causal trajectories, but in wholly contradictory ways. Often the things we most cherish were generated by what we most abhor.

As always, one question leads to others, equally problematic. In my case, a fundamental set of follow-up questions was: if freedom was not natural, not a part of the human condition, where was it first constructed, why there, and why not in all parts of the world? For me this was perhaps the most personally painful problem, one which was very nearly an intellectual crisis because it meant abandoning many cherished positions I had held earlier.

I shared the liberal tendency to assume that the values we most cherish are universal. Certainly, coming as I do from the Caribbean, and having grown up in a colonial society of predominantly African ancestry, I had been very hostile to claims by European and American intellectuals that this or that cherished ideal was peculiarly, or originally, Western. Until I came to write seriously on the subject of freedom, it seemed perverse to me that the noble struggles of colonized peoples around the world for freedom had been inspired by an ideal that they had learned from their colonial oppressors. It was far simpler to accept the still predominant Rousseauean view that to be human is to desire and know freedom; that mankind everywhere had been free and had only later been placed in chains by wicked imperialists. What insolence it was to even suggest that they needed anyone to teach them the impulse for freedom.

My profession as a sociologist reinforced my colonial, and liberal, tendency to conceive of peculiarly Western achievements in universalist terms; indeed, I rather suspect that I went into sociology partly because of this reinforcement. Sociology is a generalizing discipline. It tends to play down the particularities of culture—that is the role of the ethnographer—and instead to search for what is common in the human experience, a noble and important task, I might add. So, the growing weight of my own evidence toward the view that freedom was a peculiarly Western value, in origin and for most of its history, mightily disturbed me. I had gone into the writing of the book in the firm belief that the opposite was the case. This, after all, was clearly implicit in the basic hypothesis which drove the work: that slavery dialectically generated freedom. Since I had demonstrated in my previous work that slavery was a near universal institution, I felt confident that I would be able to show that freedom, its antithetical product, was also universal. Alas, that was not to be. This finding, this, for me, critical realization, was one of the most disturbing surprises of my career as an author.

One major problem of a more technical nature followed from these. It is the fact that writing a history of freedom, explaining its nature and origins, really amounted to writing a cultural history of the West. I had agreed with my publisher to do a book of moderate length on the subject, one of those elegant, long essays, saying everything in a hundred and sixty-two pages, which the French have so cutely, I'm sorry, acutely mastered. I soon rudely discovered that not only was I never capable of being Gallic in my style, but that the subject simply could not be treated in this essayistic manner.

Freedom was, and remains, too ingrained in the culture of the West. It permeates, and is infused by, almost all other important areas of the civilization. One simply cannot discuss it intelligently without relating it to its context. There are some subjects which simply cannot be discussed briefly. Freedom is one of them. I had not been prepared to get so deeply involved with the culture of the West, especially the ancient and medieval West, and there were times when I seriously considered giving up the whole project. Yet I persisted.

I suspect, now, that I was being propelled by deeper impulses, and it is at this point that I come to what may be called my more subconscious reasons for writing this work. Emerson once wrote that literature is the effort of Man to indemnify himself for the wrongs of his condition. There's a sense in which this work grew out of questions which were deeply rooted in my personal past, and my own social and historical background both as a Jamaican by birth, and as an African-American by choice.

As the only child of an unusually strong, one might even say overpowering, mother, with an unusually developed sense of her own freedom and independence, problems of independence, autonomy, and freedom have always been a part of my condition. She not only presented me with a model of the free person who valued her independence above all else, but forced me to sink in dependency or swim in freedom by the nature of our relationship. With a mother such as my own—and this is not the occasion to say much more on the subject—one either grew strong and free like her, or one fell crushed on the psychic wayside.

Ironically, this kind of mother-son relationship is very analogous to the relationship between colonizer and colonized, especially in the British imperial system during its passing decades. The British were an overweening colonial force, yet one which never tired of celebrating its own love of, indeed, its creation of, modern freedom. Whig, and many traditional British historians today, still interpret the history of Britain as a kind of sublime unfolding of freedom: Magna Carta, the Tudor Reformation, the Civil War, the Glorious Revolution, the Reform Act, liberalism, and all that. The British grandly, and without the slightest hint of disingenuousness, invited the colonized to learn, and to share, their commitment to freedom. But they also forced upon one the choice of becoming a conformist black Englishman or a freedom-loving, nationalist rebel.

The colonial educational system in which I was brought up deliberately rejected the traditional, Afro-Caribbean creole culture, and insisted on the assimilation of British formal culture as the price of an education. The effects of this system were not always what one might have expected. British imperial arrogance had one virtuous quality: it was extraordinarily nonpatronizing. There was no multicultural debate; you did it their way, or you did not do it at all. At the same time, if you succeeded in doing it their way, the doors of British educational culture were opened wide for you, and you were unreservedly welcomed to participate in it to whatever level your talents permitted. It was a cruel system. Most, including many who were quite talented, fell by the wayside. Those of us who succeeded all developed a love-hate relationship with British culture. To have a love-hate relationship with Britain is to have an obsessive involvement with freedom. This began from very early in the assimilative process.

Jamaica, to get back to the Emerson passage I quoted earlier, is a deeply wronged society. It was a society which had perhaps the most brutal system of slavery in the history of the modern world. It was also a slave system which had the highest incidence of large-scale revolts anywhere in the modern Americas. Much of this was simply hidden from me as a child growing up in the Anglo-Jamaican educational system, in which I acquired a thorough grounding in British history. (I was not to have my first serious course in West Indian history until the last year of high school.) That there was something different, strange, about my country's past, was hidden. It was some awful thing buried in the educational closet, and in the face of the conspiracy of silence about it in the formal educational system one tended to become aware of it in odd ways: half-remembered oral traditions passed on by old storytellers who, however, simply clammed up whenever the subject of slavery was mentioned, a trauma that could not bear remembrance; hints in folktales; the odd turn of phrase in a folksong; the occasional ruin on a sugar plantation. Within the formal educational system itself, the past and its intimate relation to slavery and freedom came upon us in the form of two holidays, the most celebrated in the annual cycle of festive days. One was Emancipation Day, August 1, when we celebrated the abolition of slavery. Of course, the British took full credit for this; little was said about actual slavery; rather, its abolition was joyfully celebrated. As the late scholar-statesman Eric Williams once wrote, the British make such a song and dance about being the first great imperial nation to abolish slavery, that one sometimes gets the impression that they imposed slavery upon the world merely for the sheer delight of abolishing it. That is not far from the truth of what happened on Emancipation Day. Apart from celebrating the magnanimity of the British we sang songs of freedom, and so the idea of freedom being emancipation for the condition of slavery was instilled in me right there, every year, as a child growing up.

But there is another day in which the same idea was reinforced, although from the opposite perspective. Empire Day was the great holiday of the year, the one in which the empire celebrated itself, and the colonized celebrated the colonizer: May 24. I have nothing but the most pleasant memories of that day: ice cream and balloons and Union Jacks waving in the sun and village bands playing British glory songs out of tune. The strangest thing about this day was the song we were all forced to sing joyously just before the national anthem: "Rule Britannia," which as you know, ends with the lines: "Britons never, never will be slaves." Many West Indians have commented on the strange effect this almost bizarrely ironic song had on them. You expect the greatest imperial nation on earth to celebrate their triumph and glory in more positive terms. It seemed to make no sense, especially to the descendants of the most brutalized slave population in modern history, that the greatest slavemongers on earth should celebrate their triumph by singing that they were not, and would never be, slaves. Whoever threatened to enslave the British? What a strange way to "bawl their liberty," as Aeschylus's Persians said of the Greeks. Looking back now, it must have been the case that the seeds of the contradictory nature of freedom were planted in my mind at that time. There had to be a reason why the greatest imperial nation on earth, the one that claimed to be freer than any other, should define their freedom to the children of their ex-slaves in so perverse a manner. What I began to learn some thirty-five years later, was that the British knew, really knew, why they sang of freedom the way they did.

And deep in our hearts, too, so did the Jamaicans. If not yet consciously and intellectually, certainly in existential sociological terms, Jamaicans understood, and continue to understand, the deep, dark dialectic of slavery and freedom. There are few societies in the world more obsessed with, more stoned on freedom, than my own. It is a ferociously libertarian place, almost chaotically freedom-loving, as numerous slave revolts, peasant revolts, class rebellions, and murderous political conflicts at election time fully attest.

My graduate education at the London School of Economics reinforced all these earlier conscious and unconscious forces that propelled me toward the argument of this work. LSE was, of course, the great liberal center of British learning, the home of Fabian socialism and of Harold Laski, the author of the single greatest volume on the history of modern freedom. To breathe the air of LSE is, I should perhaps say, was, to breathe the air of freedom. It was an atmosphere shared not only with fellow former colonials and freedom-fighters from around the old empire, but also from continental Europe. Of special importance in my journey toward this work was my early interest in French existentialist thought, more particularly, the works of Albert Camus.

I had been drawn to Camus even before going to Europe, having discovered him during my freshman year at the University of the West Indies. I read his *Myth of Sisyphus* and *The Rebel* repeatedly, perhaps obsessively, throughout my college years. I was quite taken with his notion of the absurd; it made sense to me, growing up in the thoroughly absurd world of the late colonial Jamaica. The contradictory source of meaning in the human condition, the way in which the limits of degradation define the possibilities of dignity and hope were clearly ideas that were to prove very fertile for me. Camus's own personal life growing up as a poor boy in a colonial society also intrigued me, for he had clearly been intellectually stimulated by a similar sense of strangeness and meaninglessness in the face of late colonial society. I also found his fictive portrayals of sons and lovers highly suggestive; they certainly resonated more with my experience than anything I had read in D. H. Lawrence. Finally, in *The Rebel* I found a direct exploration of the slave rebel as the archetypal starting point for a theory of freedom. As you know, Camus's reputation has declined precipitously since his premature death, and not entirely unfairly. Re-reading him today one is forced to conclude that he often pretends to be saying far more that he actually offers. For a twenty-two-year-old ex-colonial, however, he was the perfect mentor at the right time. Through him, I saw the universal possibilities in my very particular set of interests and anxieties. Hegel, to whom he drew me, might have been far more profound both in the range of his thoughts and in his celebrated treatment of slavery and freedom, but I found in Camus a soul-brother, his questionable politics and neocolonial ambivalence notwithstanding.

My long stay in Europe fully immersed me in its civilization. André Gide once wrote that we only fully conquer that which we thoroughly assimilate, and I suppose that was as good a description of my experience as any I can think of. In the midst of this inverted conquest I was also immersed in the study of my own past, writing a dissertation on slave society in Jamaica. That juxtaposition inevitably led me toward what to many may seem an absurd conclusion. I became convinced that there was only one path toward a complete understanding of my own past, my own obsessive involvement with freedom, and that was an exploration of the Western past itself, and the idea, the value, that stood at its core.

But a pleasant surprise awaited me. It has been the discovery that my own past was as useful and relevant in understanding the West as the latter has been in coming to know my own. That was one of the real joys of writing this book. There could be no better background for an understanding of the ancient West than that of the West Indian, or more broadly, that of the African-American. The West began in the alienating storm of large-scale slavery. Its greatness springs from the dialectic between outsider and insider, master and slave, the native and the foreigner, colonizer and colonized.

Bearing in mind the present debate over multiculturism and Afrocentrism, I would like to close by suggesting that in a fascinating, perhaps perverse, way the group of people whose experience is most pertinent to the ancient and medieval world, and who need most to understand that world if they are to understand themselves, are black Americans and blacks of the diaspora. Because we are the people closest to the dialectic of slavery and freedom, we are closer to the generative core of Western culture. No group of people have a greater existential intimacy with this most complex, most perverse, most consuming of ideals. Which is to say no group of people are better placed to understand, and are more in need of understanding, the early history of the West. Discovering this has been the most important part of writing *Freedom.*

Orlando Patterson

THE WRITING LIFE

After *Mating* came out and was to my immense surprise so generously received, I found myself being asked more questions than I'm used to answering. Readers and interviewers wanted to know a lot about me. The questions fell into two categories, one easy and the other unexpectedly hard. The easy ones were variants of the question *"How* do you write?" and comprehended queries about my work habits, what writing machine I use (an antique manual typewriter), where I get my ideas and especially where I got the idea I could write a novel in the feminine first person, and whether I had found it arduous writing a narrative without using quotation marks or giving a name to my narrator.

The array of harder questions constellated as *"Why* do you write?" or more precisely, "Why do you write this *kind* of book and why did you write this book in particular?" As I attempted to give good-faith answers to this strain of question, I realized I hadn't asked myself such questions in many years. I have always felt a compulsion to write. I've never wanted or intended to be anything but a writer. I realized that for a very long time I'd been proceeding from literary project to literary project, each one of which seemed, as I undertook it, certain to justify the fixated effort that would go into its completion. And I had always pushed a substantial backlog of projects ahead of me. It became apparent to me that the answers I was giving to the question of why I write were inadequate—not exactly evasive, but only partially responsive. So I made myself think more radically on the matter. The result of these ponderings is what I chiefly want to present to you here—along with answers to the easier question of how I write, as opportunities arise. Fair answers to the questions in these two columns should go some way toward filling the space controlled by the heading "The Writing Life." As we proceed, I hope to draw out the most generalizable implications of my self-interrogation. "How fascinating is that class / Whose only member is Me!" W. H. Auden wrote.[1] I'll be unhappy if, when I conclude, those lines sum up my efforts here.

First, let me sketch the writing life I've had. Obviously it hasn't been a writing life in the sense that Henry James, say, had one. What I've had, until the last few years, is a life where—like most writers—I've managed to write in the margins of making a living and rearing a family. I've supported myself by selling used books, teaching, working in Africa as codirector (with my wife Elsa) of a Peace Corps program. I write serious fiction. The industry term for the kind of novel *Mating* is, "literary novel," seemed like a redundancy to me on first hearing. What it means is that sales exceeding fifteen thousand copies for this kind of book would be extraordinary—and in fact the first printing of M*ating* was for just that: fifteen thousand.

I've been scribbling assiduously since I was a young boy. When I was eleven I included a feuilleton picaresque novel, *A Modern Buccaneer*, in the pages of the *Town Crier*, a newspaper I printed on a gelatin duplicator and hawked door-to-door in the Oakland, California, suburb I grew up in. Under the spell of Chesterton's Father Brown stories I created my own genius detective, Doctor Orion Curme, who physically resembled Father Brown but who was a proselytizing atheist. I sacrificed a couple of summer vacations to the writing and illustrating of twenty or so Doctor Curme stories. In junior high I wrote a novel which was the purported journal of Phra, the Phoenician, who was, incidentally, another pirate hero. I went to prison in 1951 as a war resister, wangled a night job in the prison boilerhouse, and used the small hours to write a mock-Conradian novel about a group of high-minded adventurers losing their lives in a doomed nonviolent scheme intended to overthrow a bestial Central American dictator by the name of Larco Tur.

I believe I thought I was pioneering a promising and morally instructive new genre, that of the nonviolent thriller. When my parole was granted, after I'd spent nine months in the minimum-security prison in Tucson, it was brought home to me that I was forbidden to take any prison writings with me on release; I could only take the cards and letters that had been sent to me. I was determined to get my novel out, somehow, and I terrified the very decent man who was my only authorized visitor with the proposition that on his next visit I secrete the carefully rolled up manuscript (I wrote on both sides of each page) in the tube in the toilet paper roll in the bathroom used both by prisoners and visitors and that he smuggle it out for me. He was a brave man and even though he was a lawyer, an officer of the court, he tremblingly agreed to do it. I'm happy to say that I reread the novel and decided it might not be worth the risk he would bear. So I copied the entire manuscript over in an even more microscopic hand on small squares of onion skin paper which I affixed in layers to the undersides of the flaplike winter scenes on my top-of-the-line Christmas cards. No one bothered, as I left, to look through my collection of rather chubby Christmas cards, nor was anyone at pains even to open up the manila envelope containing my correspondence. Back in Oakland I read my novel yet again, decided it was derivative, and threw it out. After college (Swarthmore 1956) I began to publish highly sporadically in literary quarterlies. I produced a sequence of experimental, abstract, excruciatingly self-referential novellas (all unpublished), then began to revise my approach to writing in the direction of plainness. I wrote an unpublished bildungsroman (*Equals*), began to publish in *The New Yorker*, went to Africa for five years, where it was possible only to take notes for future writing. On our return I received my first grants and fellowships, published my collection of African stories, *Whites,* in 1986, and published *Mating* in 1991. The rest, one might say, is very recent history. I've been able to write full-time since 1984.

In my writing life, the intent to aim at high art emerged relatively early, not long after I'd passed through the last of my periods of self-instruction through imitation. For me, the high art of the serious novel, and of the serious short story, consists in supreme realizations of other lives—presentations of other, imagined lives, or parts of lives, variously angled, cropped, elongated, arranged with aesthetic cunning designed to elucidate the uniqueness and significance of the particular life or lives recounted. I advance this as a stipulation, for the purposes of getting on with what I have to say, although I'm always prepared to defend this contention. This presentation of selves in high art lies at the farthest point on the literary spectrum from the presentations characteristic of genre, or as they are now called, "category," novels or stories—that is, of those works which make up the vast preponderance of fiction in the modern era and whose general aim is opposite to the aims of high art, category fiction being contrived to bring the reader into repetitive and formulaic experiences, versions of the already established. After I say more about the origins of my own passion to create seriously imagined lives, I want to say something about the companion passion to enter the lives imagined in high art, the passion of the serious reader.

People become writers dedicated to high art for all kinds or reasons. Some become writers because no one will listen, or in order to propagandize, or for revenge, or to get respect, or to redo symbolically their own lives (it's amusing to note how frequently the heroes or heroines of novels turn out to be roughly the same age as their creator and to have the same syllabic count in their names as he or she does). The list looks endless. For all intending writers, there is the allure of the contest with the dead masters, the invitation to demonstrate intelligence, artfulness, excellence. The correct psychological term for my impulsion toward writing would be, I think, "filial-pietistic," which refers to the carrying out of the perceived life-project of a dominant parent, the replication of it if the project has been successful or the completion of it if it has been thwarted. I think I probably began to write because my father didn't, or wouldn't. He wanted to. And it isn't quite true that he didn't, which I'll explain. My birth in 1933 precipitated my father's abandonment of his vocation up until then as a trade union organizer and as the California state secretary of the Socialist party. The San Francisco General Strike of 1934, in which he was an activist, was the last straw for my mother, who issued an ultimatum. The scene would make a good one-act play, for which the title could be *Birth of a Salesman*. My father opened a job-printing shop, went broke at that, and then became a salesman, and finally a master trainer of salesmen. As a boy, he had written poetry under the pseudonym Silenus Starset. As a man, for a while, he wrote Whitmanesque protest poetry which appeared in a little journal he published called *The Rebel*: this journal was circulated through an organization, the National Amateur Press Association, consisting of people who had adopted amateur status not because they had failed to get published in the usual way but apparently because they had concluded they wouldn't have been published in the usual way if they'd tried. I witnessed the devolution, as I certainly saw it, of my father's core allegiances, which took him from free thought and democratic socialism, through liberal Protestantism, and finally to the wilder shores of Rosicrucianism. As a child, I remember my father chanting John G. Neihardt's "Cry of the People" in the bathroom as he prepared to go to work:

Tremble before thy chattels,
Lords of the scheme of things!
Fighters of all earth's battles,
Ours is the might of kings!
Guided by seers and sages,
The world's heart-beat for a drum,
Snapping the chains of ages,
Out of the night we come!

Lend us no ear that pities!
Offer no almoner's hand!
Alms for the builders of cities!
When will you understand?
Down with your pride of birth
And your golden gods of trade!
A man is worth to his mother, Earth,
All that a man has made!

We are the workers and makers!
We are no longer dumb!
Tremble, O Shirkers and Takers!
Sweeping the earth—we come!
Ranked in the world-wide dawn,
Marching into the day!
The night is gone and the sword is drawn
And the scabbard is thrown away![2]

Toward the end of his life he would sit in the dark and chant vowel
sounds in certain configurations supposed to attract angelic beings.

The trick on me was that he abandoned his original definition of
himself before I had much chance to react against it, which left me with
little choice but somehow to honor it. I considered the library he

assembled in early manhood to be the residue of his true self: it contained works by Zola, Erskine Caldwell, Frank Norris, James T. Farrell, Upton Sinclair, and, behind glass doors and a lock which I mastered, D. H. Lawrence, *The Sexual Life of Savages,* and racily illustrated limited editions of Rabelais and two Defoe classics, *Moll Flanders* and *Roxana the Fortunate Mistress.* In these last two works, it has very recently occurred to me, lay the implication that a good way, maybe even the best way, for a man to write a book, was in the voice of an indomitable woman. Since these books were locked up, they—I must have concluded—were the truest, because the most dangerous. (Let me not scant the contribution to the general deification of art made by my mother and her side of the family. There, it was all singing, all dancing. My mother is a lyric soprano who trained lengthily for an operatic career she was never to achieve. Her family survived the worst of the Great Depression through employment in a marionette theater organized by my Uncle Ralph. Two of my siblings have been songwriters. Among my maternal aunts and cousins are or were actors, stage directors, self-taught lute- and harpsichord-makers, modern dancers, sculptors, and puppeteers.) An odd thing is that when I began to publish, my father showed almost no interest in my work. This surprised me.

So much for the main subliminal prompting that led to my determination to become a writer. Or perhaps I should say "partly subliminal," since it was a matter for open allusion in our family that I, personally, through being born and costing a lot to raise, had aborted my father's original more heroic mixed vocation of writing and social revolt. The allusions were rueful and not punitive in any way. We all accepted it.

Of course, once I'd begun to write, and as I moved deeper into the world of books, all the usual impulses that will sustain the drive to write declared themselves. Increasingly, I wanted to write because literature meant liberation to me, liberation from the thrall of my own personal cast of demons. And what nobler life-objective could there be than qualifying myself as an affiliate of those who, from their resting places in the stacks of the Melrose Library, had helped me convert alienation into productive autonomy?

The conviction that I could add something distinctly my own to the deep appreciation of lives lived in my time grew not with the success of my literary efforts but with the strengthening both of my craft and of my sense that subtle yet enormous changes were coming virtually unremarked into the way we live now. Being in Africa for five years drastically intensified all my impulses to capture life as I saw it there, pursuant to the sudden shift in the relationship between figure and ground that finding oneself "altogether elsewhere" (W. H. Auden) so often yields.

Finally, beyond the intent commandingly to present lives which in new ways summarize and embody previously unevoked aesthetic and moral themes and conclusions, there is another aspiration, which is one day to find that one's work, through luck or inspiration, has, in the manner of a fractal, managed to condense truths about the condition of being human that transcend the boundaries of time and place within which one has chosen consciously to work. This is a prize that is almost never won.

I'd like now to consider the civic dimensions of the act of writing seriously, of writing serious fiction in particular, and to look concurrently at the worsening siege conditions affecting the place where all writing is done. Several tendencies in our culture are grimly menacing to the future of the book, all books, not excluding the most narrowly technical and utilitarian. Most conspicuously, there is the persistence of illiteracy and the growth of paraliteracy. The statistics are oppressive—thirty-six million adult Americans reading at an eighth-grade level or below—and the causes track back to defects in formal education, to deterioration in educative processes within families, and to the de-skilling effects flowing from the rise of competitive visual media—the electronic media preeminently, with their commercially driven bias toward shallow amusement, repetition (again), interruptability, generic amiability, amnesis, and the micro-division of units of presentation. Additionally, the forces favoring censorship are growing bolder, drawing sustenance from the old and new political and religious fundamentalisms currently asserting themselves. And then there is the sheer, brute crowding out of books by cultural substitutes whose use requires less energy and less attention. In this connection, I briefly quote from a recent study touching on this development. This is from Neil Postman's *Amusing Ourselves to Death*:

> From Erasmus in the sixteenth century to Elizabeth Eisenstein in the twentieth, almost every scholar who has grappled with the question of what reading does to one's habits of mind has concluded that the process encourages rationality; that the sequential, propositional character of the written word fosters what Walter Ong calls the "analytic management of knowledge."[3]

Nasty synergies emerge. Negative tendencies reinforce one another over time. Illiteracy cohabits with television, even as television—recent research shows—weakens the ability of young brains to access the riches encoded in text. Political discourse suffers in all this, and not only because language and thus expressive competence are in decline; worse, the dominance of visual media of the kind we seem to have created for ourselves leads to a translocation of political contestation away from argument and toward a witless competition among images. A muffled panic in the public results, manifesting itself sometimes as apathy, sometimes as support for various of the fundamentalisms—religious, political, cultural-political as in identity politics— whose essential maneuver is to make the world more agreeable by curtailing the flow of cultural material disquieting to their followerships. It hardly needs to be emphasized that this weakening of political discourse, and thereby of the self-renewing capacities of our democracy, comes at a bad time. We seem to be entering what looks very much like a general crisis of the present global dispensation, extending even to the natural systems on which social survival is premised. In defending books, we defend the critical powers potentiated by them. None of the above is news, really, but it's important that we remain aware of the gravity of our predica-ment. Consider how difficult it seems to be for even those economic entities like newspapers of record and weekly news magazines—entities directly dependent on a continuing, broadly based public capacity to read competently—how difficult it seems to be for them to grasp the degree to which they abet the tendencies undoing them: the *New York Times* has recently eliminated the book review column in its Saturday editions, and both *Time* and *Newsweek* now occasionally entirely skip coverage of the world of books. Throughout the daily press the length and number of book reviews are steadily declining, and the process of reviewing is yielding almost everywhere to pressures to make stars or letter-grades or some other reductive ranking device a part of the review.

In closing, I'd like to concentrate on the particular civic functions of serious fiction, and to link myself with those who identify the drive to read it and write it as fundamentally ethical in character. Why is the serious reader drawn again and again to the interminable parade of imagined lives kept marching forth by writers and publishers? We are, I think, seeking some elusive thing or outcome, something answering to a need stronger than the voyeurism or curiosity or desire for distraction that may lead us to any book initially.

I think we would like to love our species, if we could. And I think that if we are even a little educated, we know how limited is our individual ability to see around or through the influences that have shaped our powers to understand the world and ourselves. We resemble, individually, sufferers from agnosia, a perceptual disorder whose victims are able to identify the properties of an object without being able to recognize what the object is. We know that we each arrive in the world wearing the infinitely fine net custom-woven for us by the Fates, a net whose knots tighten each time we step off the track that has been preselected for us. We can love our species because we are ordered to by the spiritual director of our choice, or we can attempt, by passing through the alternative lives serious fiction brings us, to assemble a truer composite of what we are, with the intent of discovering, in the process, to what degree we should enlarge or qualify the baffled unformed sympathy we begin with. In stories or the novel we are privileged to enjoy the least constrained representation of life achievable in any communicative form. Expository writing can't help but declare its viewpoint, and we normally know the bearing of the real lives presented in biography and autobiography before we begin, because the reputation of the subject alerts us. In serious fiction, we are able to enter disarmed and to open ourselves to the healthy subversions produced by the truth told excessively and beautifully and from vantage points different from our own and different from one another. Truth is a product of collabora-tion. We writers know it, and that's why, despite the ineliminably rivalrous atmosphere in which we work, we feel ourselves uplifted—for a time, anyway—by the occasional triumphs of our peers in seizing and displaying a life that tells us things no life has told us before.

These are large claims for literature, I know, but the iron compul-sion of the different fundamentalisms to suppress or stigmatize whole classes of imagined lives suggests to me that I'm correct. Proletcult, a mass movement in the Russia of 1919, dismissed all literature produced before 1917 as bourgeois—Chekhov, Turgenev, Tolstoy, Pushkin, no exceptions. The local Proletcult chapter in Tambov planned to burn all the books in the libraries "in the belief that the shelves would refill on the first of the new year with nothing but proletarian works," as Richard Stites records.[4] In Nazi Germany, as we all know, it was the test of Aryanness that imagined lives had to pass. We have had the Index Prohibitorum and we have with us today the international death sentence pronounced on Salman Rushdie by the Ayatollah Ruhollah Khomeini, whose ascent to power Michel Foucault, in a spectacular display of agnosia, welcomed as "the eruption of the sacred into modernity."

I think this is a good place to finish. I hope I've shed some light on the enterprise of writing serious fiction. And I hope I've suggested persuasively that serious fiction has utilities we ignore at our own peril.

In 1931 Virginia Woolf drafted a speech for delivery to a group of professional women. It contains a sentence I say to myself whenever I speak in public, as a stimulus to brevity. She wrote: "The best men can do is not to talk about themselves any more." The time is long past due for me to comply. Good night and thank you for your gracious attention.

Norman Rush

Notes

1. All quotations from W. H. Auden are from Auden, *The Collected Poems* (New York: Vintage Books, 1991).

2. John G. Neihardt, "Cry of the People," from *The Giving Earth: A John G. Neihardt Reader*, edited by Hilda Neihardt Petri (Lincoln and London: University of Nebraska Press, 1991), pp. 17-18. Used by permission of the University of Nebraska Press.

3. Neil Postman, *Amusing Ourselves to Death: Public Discourse in the Age of Show Business* (New York: Viking, 1985), p. 51.

4. Richard Stites, *Revolutionary Dreams: Utopian Vision and Experimental Life in the Russian Revolution* (New York: Oxford University Press, 1989), p. 71.

ACKNOWLEDGMENTS

The Board of Directors of the National Book Foundation gratefully acknowledges the support of the following donors for National Book Week 1992: the American Booksellers Association, the Association of American Publishers, Book-of-the-Month Club, Inc., the Lila Wallace–Reader's Digest Fund, the New York State Council on the Arts, and Random House, Inc./S.I. Newhouse Foundation.

C O L O P H O N

Type

Helvetica and Times

Composition

Created electronically using Aldus Pagemaker®
on the Apple® Macintosh® computer
by Franklin Street Communications, Inc.

Cover Paper

Mohawk Superfine Softwhite Regular Finish 80#

Text Paper

Mohawk Superfine Softwhite Eggshell Finish 80#

Printing

Garamond Pridemark Press, Inc.
Baltimore, Maryland

Illustration

Derived from *Planisphere céleste* (Paris: N. de Fer, 1731)

Design

Franklin Street Communications, Inc.
Richmond, Virginia